THE DIARY OF A
Single Mom

THE DIARY OF A
Single Mom

Browniesha M. Blackman

Copyright © 2023 by Browniesha M. Blackman

Cover by Preetu Trivedi
Edited by Sierra C. Campbell

Love Wins Publishing
Chandler, Arizona
www.lovewinspub.com

All rights reserved. This book or any portion thereof may not be reproduced or used in any manner whatsoever without the express written permission of the publisher or the author except for the use of brief quotations in a book review.

Printed in the United States of America
First Printing, May 2023

"Being a mother is learning about strengths you didn't know you had."

Being a mother is one of the highest unpaid positions. There is no financial payment to receive. The compensation is love from a tiny human being who will one day become an adult. Over that period of time the maternal love only grows.

One topic that is not often talked about in motherhood is grief. There are so many forms of grief. Grieving the fact that maybe you just can't give your kids the world, grieving the fact that you did all you could with what you had, grieving the fact that one day they will leave home. Let's not forget grieving that little girl or boy who now is an adult in a relationship.

Whew! Motherhood!!

There is one form of grief that is felt that no mother ever desires to feel and that's the loss of a child.

I dedicate this book to Roshanda Casteel and her late son Elijah E. Rufus who transitioned while this project was being completed. Words are ineffable. Being a mother sometimes comes with speechless & painful moments. This is one moment that none of us could ever prepare for.

Browniesha M. Blackman

From Roshanda Casteel

In loving memory of

Elijah E. Rufus
June 26, 2003 – February 15, 2023

Elijah E. Rufus passed away at the youthful age of 19 years old on February 15, 2023. Words cannot express the way I feel. The love and memories of the many good times we shared are truly a blessing to have.

To continue the legacy of my son Elijah, I have started the **Elijah E. Rufus Nu Pathway Foundation** for at-risk youth and foster children, ages 18-25 years old. The mission was to make sure that teenagers who were aging out of the foster system would have continuous support, guidance, inspiration, housing, funding and more.

www.thelifeofelijahrufus.com

Elijah and I both have had our own experience with the foster care system. We wanted to create opportunities beyond the standard of this system. Through the **Elijah E. Rufus Nu Pathway**, so many teenagers and young adults will be provided a substantial amount of support that will never be misleading or misguided. Our mission is to reunify and restore relationships and be the light in a dark place.

Dear Diary,

Today is Monday, and the day didn't start off so great. For the past three months, I've been working a graveyard schedule. I didn't take into account the effect that it would have on my body or the effect that it would have on my children due to me having to pick them up from my mom's house at 4:30 am in the morning.

It has been extremely hard for all of us. We get home around 5:30 am. I put them in bed only to wake them up two hours later to get them ready for school. I'm so overwhelmed and stressed. Why do I have to do this alone? When I originally thought about working the graveyard schedule, I thought it was the best option because I could drop them off and pick them up from school and make dinner before heading to work.

Christmas is coming up, and I wanted to make some extra cash. I'm a small business owner, so I wanted to make sure I had enough money to make sure Christmas was good for them. As a mom, one of the most important things is making sure my babies are taken care of. I'm not sure how much longer this is gonna last because it is starting to be extremely hard. Some days I am so tired, or they are so tired that they don't even get to go to school. I had to call off work a few times because I couldn't even make it from being exhausted. Sometimes I sit and cry because I just want things to be right for my babies. It's all on me, and I'm only one person trying to show up for them and me. As I said, I am a small business owner, and sometimes, sales are slow. Sometimes you make money, and sometimes you don't. This means working a 9 to 5 is the best thing for me right now.

We often hear that God will not give us more than we can bear. I sometimes doubt that, but I know that God will get me through.
If I'm being honest, I don't fully show up for my babies sometimes because I am so exhausted with

my own stuff. Trying to pay bills, going to work, and making sure that they have everything they need. I miss moments in their life. It is hard feeling like you missed out on your kids' life just because you want to make life better for them.

One thing I know is that they love me, they see my hard work, and they show me that they appreciate it. There have been times when I have fallen asleep on the couch, and my daughter would put a blanket over me. Or my son would see how exhausted I am and rub my back. I thank God for giving me my babies.

We're like the Three Musketeers. I love my little, broke best friends. I know the journey can be hard, but it's worth it. I know our foundation is built on prayer. I've taught my children how to pray, and I know that, even though it looks hard or feels overwhelming, there's a greater purpose at the end of it all.

Dear Diary,

I'm tired...

But I keep going. What else am I supposed to do?

I am alive but most days I don't feel like I'm living. I'm in survival mode. I've been in this mode for more than 24 years, when I had my first child as a *single* mother.

I was 17 years old. He was 27. I had no business being with him. Hell, he had no business being with me. I lied about my age though. I told him I was 18. Even then he should have left me alone.

Ultimately, he left me alone anyway because I raised our son by myself. In hindsight, I can't say he didn't try to be involved. I just wish he would have tried harder for the sake of our son who is struggling now as a result.

It wasn't until recently that I realized the value and importance of a father. I didn't have my dad around, so I didn't think I needed his dad around, especially when things went sour in our situationship.

I found out he was married when our son was two months old. I was devastated. I took it hard. Even though they clearly weren't living together, I would spend weekends with him at his house. He would leave me there alone. We paged one another and talked all times of the night when we weren't physically together. I thought he was my man. I had no clue he was married!

It was hard to break away from him. He sure didn't make it easy. He bought me a diamond ring, continued pursuing me for sex, spent time with me and our son... It was a lot and quite confusing at 19 years old.

Somewhere I found the courage and strength to

say enough was enough though. I decided to move forward raising our son by myself. I mean, I dated here and there but no one was allowed around my son. I wanted companionship. I wanted a partner, and I wanted help. Who wants to raise a child alone?!

Dear Diary,

Some of the hardest days are when you realize you don't have enough money to make ends meet. It's about one of the most frustrating days you can have. Just the thought of not having it all together to make things happen for your kids is difficult.

Being a single mom can be very hard. Sometimes you have days where you just have to sit in your car and cry. Some days you show up with a smile on your face in spite of everything going wrong. You will walk around with that smile, your kids unaware of things being out of place. Yes, that's your responsibility as a mother, but that doesn't mean it doesn't hurt.

I'm praying for better days because I know God is faithful to his word. I know that His promises are yes and amen. I know he said that he'd never leave me, nor will he forsake me. I know that he said he'd go before me and make every crooked path straight. So, I have to hold onto his unchanging hand. I gotta believe that he's going to change the situation with my finances.

He's looking down on me. He knows I tried my best, but the truth is, it's hard for me. Even when I try my best, I just do not have enough money.

Dear Diary,

I don't think single parenthood has ever been the ideal situation for any woman. A handbook could have made it all so simple. At least I would have had the option to follow it or even implement a modified version according to what I learned growing up. I would have extracted learned behaviors from childhood that were unhealthy, sprinkled a little of my own morals and values inside, with a side of healthy boundaries, and had the best recipe.

Being a mom is like making gumbo. You apply so many theories when raising children as you combine many different ingredients in the gumbo pot. The roux is the base and determines the richness of the flavor. With motherhood, the foundation set for your children will determine their character as adults as well as their likelihood of being independent citizens.

I learned this and so much more about being a mother when I became pregnant at seventeen and in the 12th grade. I guess it doesn't have to be such bad news. When I played house as a kid, I never pretended to be the baby momma of an inmate, but here I am.

Most little girls imagine growing up, getting married, and having the perfect family. You know, like the television families - the Cosby family being my favorite example. They lived so much like the family I remember as a kid. Dr. Huxtable was always present to provide and protect, while the Mrs. assisted with teachings of love. But I learned very early in life that this is not always the case.

Some parents are actually not prompted to grow up once they become parents. This is commonly true when people are too young to assume these roles. It can be a disaster if they aren't taught the responsibilities of being a parent. I see far more moms taking their jobs seriously, while many dads make babies but remain immature and complacent. Look at my baby's daddy. He thinks it's cute to have a little person who looks like him while undermining the sacrifice it requires to be a parent. He's so busy hanging in the streets with his so-called friends that he doesn't have time for what should now be his main priority. It wasn't until jail that we became his greatest consistency.

He consistently calls and requests things, sometimes things we barely have. I don't think he understands the position he has put us in now that he is gone. What about his lack of consistency with the physical and emotional needs of my children that will one day show up as childhood trauma?

Raising my daughter was like emotional therapy because we were girls learning and growing together. Every moment of all my days was filled with her company, activities, and interests. I never really felt off balance as a single mom until I added the boys into the equation. I became one foot in at dance class and one foot in at soccer practice, cheer, football... I'm sure you get the picture. If an octopus were human, it could now be me. My mom is such a lifesaver. Whenever I need her to step in, she does just that.

Astrology doesn't reign over my life, but they say Sagittarians are loyal to a default. This seems true of me since I always decide to answer the collect calls from jail. I answered them for ten years. But weekend jail visits and phone conversations become tedious when Saturdays are dedicated to grocery shopping, laundry, and family time. Being a parent has its challenges, and when you're doing it by yourself, you really tend to be hard on yourself. It sends you into a survival mode that men will never understand.

After three children and a shit load of single mom chronicles, I could write a book of the do's and don'ts. You must know who you are in order to be in charge of another human being. While this may sound insane, being a single mom has great benefits. You gain a sense of accomplishment like steamrolling any other obstacle. It is not the end of the world, and it breaks common stereotypes.

Yes, I have seen a woman raise successful men all by themselves. I probably feel different about being a single mom than most. It molded me, laced me, strengthened me, challenged me, acknowledged me, and grew me. If I wouldn't have become a parent and the baby momma of an inmate, I know some of the roads I traveled would have been less bumpy. As I recall those times, I realize that it was a period of healthy silence in my life. Those were times that motivated some of my greatest achievements as a woman and mother.

Dear Diary,

When I became a single mother, it came with a fight. I had my newborn child snatched from my arms from the man that was my baby's daddy. I was in my last year of high school and had to leave my parents' home at the bright age of 18. I had to move in with my baby's dad to get my child back. I was told I would never get my baby back if I didn't move in with him.

So, I left my parent's home and moved in with him. I was not going to let another woman – or person – put their hands on my baby. I lived in his home until I was about 24 years old. By that time, my second child had been born, and I was married to my children's father. But my entire time living in his home was unsafe.

I lived in the midst of drugs, alcohol, guns, sex, women, threats, and more. There was never any togetherness with the one that I loved so much.

Most of the time, when a woman has a child with a man, there are deep feelings of love and joy. For me, that love was never reciprocated; at least, it was never deeply expressed. So, I never knew whether he loved me or not.

As the years went by, I experienced a lot of mental and emotional abuse by this man, but never any physical abuse. I was told, however, that if I left him, he would kill me. After hearing those words, the spirit of fear and procrastination followed me for a very long time. I began to understand that you can be a married woman and still hold the 'single mom' title. I was single and expected to do everything that a single mom should do without help from the other parent. Therefore, I made the decision to make my single mom status official.

After coming home from work one Sunday, I saw my babies in the care of another woman's sister while their dad sat in the living room, socializing with friends. He had even refused to take me to work or pick me up. I had to walk down the street to a childhood friend's home to get a ride to work. I was charged fifty dollars that I didn't even have. I was so embarrassed because fifty dollars was equal to one of my checks.

So, we got into a verbal altercation, and I stood my ground. I went across the street to a friend's house and called the police so that I could pack up my babies and my things and move out safely. I called my parents, and my dad brought me one of their cars to move our things out of the house and move back home with them.

I was blackmailed by my children's dad. He threatened to report me to the job and to Child Protective Family Service if I didn't come back to him. Of course, I refused to return and continued to declare my single mom status.

I had to be a single mom to my babies, even while

with my husband. I was separated from him because he had a child with another woman. My single mom status helped me be free from a nightmare I didn't know was possible.

My advice to other single mothers would be to stay strong and never allow anyone to make you feel unworthy. Be who you are and do what you must to make sure you and your babies are safe. My true freedom came when I got to know who God was and what he could do for me.

Dear Diary

I was never supposed to raise my sons by myself. I'm trying to wrap my head around how I got here. With more than 20 years of parenting, it's all hitting differently now.

My youngest is 14. He's a great kid. Very smart. Witty. Sharp. Inquisitive. Funny.... And socially awkward. He has no care about his appearance and although I try to teach him, what do I know?

Today while trying to shop for new shoes, I felt like a failure of a mom. I know it sounds crazy, but we were both walking around the department store clueless. For years, I picked his clothes and his shoes and if you know me you know I have no style or fashion sense at all. All I know is to make sure it's clean and color coordinated for the most part. Apparently, I've passed that on to him.

My older son is an adult. He had to figure his fashion style out as well. He's another story altogether.

In shopping for shoes for my 14-year-old, I realized how I didn't really *raise* my sons. I survived and they survived with me. Where I thought I was teaching them I was really just surviving. I went to work and school. I still go to work and school. Somewhere I was programmed that an education would help me position myself better financially. For the record, I'm better positioned yet still struggling.

I am literally on autopilot. I wake up, roll out the bed, get the day going, work until I can't think straight and when I get home, I'm so tired I'm crawling into bed for a nap that often becomes me falling asleep on top of the covers still clothed.

I change clothes when I get home so I'm not on my bed in street clothes (something my granny taught me) but some days I make it to the shower before I "nap" into the next day and some days the shower is my morning kiss. But overall, I go hard because I have to .

As we looked at shoes trying to find something *he* likes and can fit, I thought " *This is something his dad should be doing.*" I texted two of my guy friends for advice on where to go to find decent shoes for boys, well a man, because he wears a size 14 shoe, and where we were wasn't working. That's when it hit me, and I nearly passed out in the department store.

I was never supposed to be doing this on my own. I was married to his father. He begged me for a baby, so I got off birth control. It was a matter of months before I was pregnant. I was young and fertile. We were married and happy. So, I thought.

Dear Diary,

Being a single mother of two had its advantages and disadvantages. It was a struggle living on a fixed income. While on public assistance – or welfare – I had to budget.

I would pay rent and any other bills and buy one child a pair of shoes and the other one an outfit, and the next month vice versa. I made sure my babies had what they needed. I was able to buy what I needed every three to six months, but sometimes I would go without.

But having God on my side helped. He made it happen for my babies and me. As a child, God gave my mom a formula while we received assistance for a short period of time. The Lord helped me remember, and I used that formula. From the 1st to the 15th of each month, prices would be extremely high in stores. After that, the prices would go down. So, when I got my food stamps, I started buying groceries that we needed to last through those days and saved the rest. I would wait for the prices to go back to normal, then go buy what we really needed, and sometimes wanted, to stock the cabinets.

God sustained us and took care of us; we never went without. Psalm 23 became alive: "The LORD is my shepherd; I shall not want."

Dear Diary,

I am sitting here trying to figure out where to start. When I first became a mom, I had no idea I would become a single mom. I was embarrassed and ashamed because I felt like I had let my parents, grandmother, and God down. I had an excellent support team from my family, but the shame set in after my relationship ended.

It was over before she was born, but I did my best to make it work. After the breakup, he told me no man would want to be in a committed relationship with me other than for sex because I already had a child. I was brokenhearted because he seemed different from the other guys. I preferred gangsters or drug dealers.

In my relationships, I have been through verbal abuse, physical abuse, and cheating. It is hard being a mother. Mothers play many roles in raising children, single or married. I know that motherhood does not come with instructions. It's just learning as you go. I have made so many mistakes that I cannot undo them.

Being a mother of eight – with one child dying after birth – with five different men has been a sign that I have issues when it comes to relationships. I will admit there have been times when I wished I wasn't a mom. It is challenging and can become physically and mentally draining. I have done things that I could never admit, things I regret. There are times I have felt like they would have been better off if I wasn't their mother. They have had to deal with a lot of things because of my lifestyle.

Being a mother is also a privilege, but being a grandmother gave me another chance to improve my skills. The relationship between me and my grandkids has been a great experience that warms my heart.

As I type these words, I am filled with shame, disappointment, guilt, and regret when thinking of my mistakes, primarily my two failed marriages. After my son's father went to prison on a life sentence, I thought my life was over. We had many hopes and dreams of opening another business, buying a home, and escaping our dangerous lifestyle. Now after his thirty-one-year sentence, he is home. We have a great friendship, and I realized I still love him even more than before he left.

Looking over my life, I made mistakes, but I have also made some remarkable accomplishments over the past 19 years. I pray that whoever reads this knows that God gives second chances. Despite any mistakes you make, please ask your child or children for forgiveness. The blessing for me is that I still have love from my children, who I love with all my heart.

Dear Diary,

Being a single mom has been very difficult at times, especially when it comes to money. I didn't always know what to do with the money that I was blessed with. I made a lot of mistakes partially because I wasn't consistent in managing my finances, wasting money on things that had little value.

As a young, single black mom, we were not always given many options. I remember asking other young mothers around my age how they managed their money. There was not much of a response because we were all struggling to survive while taking care of our babies. Some of those struggles led to me being on public assistance and getting help from the housing authority and food pantries, which was the norm for single mothers at that time. Who wants to spend a lifetime getting assistance from these places? I didn't; I always strived for better.

I was living paycheck to paycheck, trying to make ends meet. Getting food stamps certainly helped with the food.

One time, I got laid off from work and had to file for bankruptcy twice. This definitely wasn't fun. When they came out with payday loans, I found myself in one to three places at a time. That was truly a nightmare when I couldn't pay the loan back. I would just wait until the place called me. Then, I would be put on a payment plan until the loan was paid in full.

The single mom life came with many challenges, but I learned how to persevere and stand with my faith in God. I believed he would see me through. I had to learn how to grip that solid rock to keep me strong in many areas of my life. I found that there is a light at the end of the tunnel.

After many ups and downs with money, I got tired of years of failure. My lack of money was not allowing me to live up to my full potential. So, I decided to fight back and put the spirit of failure to rest. The Bible says that money answers all things. Ecclesiastes 10:19 says, *"A feast is made for laughter, and wine maketh merry: but money answereth all things."*

I wanted my money to answer for me. I ended up finding an extra job and going back to school to further my education. I even started a small business from my home. I got busy and started putting the pen and paper to good use. I budgeted and wrote down my income, the bills I had to pay, and the debt I had to pay off.

I had to be very persistent and not give up. This helped me with investing and putting money into an emergency fund. Make sure you never leave yourself broke and dry. I thank God every day for his help and never take it for granted. I encourage all single mothers – young and old – to never give up.

Dear Diary,

I am a proud mother of seven amazing children.

As a mother, I find myself praying for direction and praying for understanding. Not just because I was a single mother, but I knew that I was going to need some help because there wasn't any consistency in the relationship that I was in with my ex-husband.

What I've learned over the years is that life has a way of just happening. So many things that we experience are definitely unexpected. And in some situations, we even have children who were definitely a part of the plan, but we learn how to trust God throughout the process, and he has never failed me yet.

I've always had challenges and communication barriers with my parents, but I was blessed to have a great grandmother, who was rooted in faith, and had a firm foundation and trust in God, and she definitely made a point to make sure that He was a part of my life in every way possible.

She was an amazing example of a woman, but most importantly, she showed the strength of what it took to be a successful mother. That was powerful and inspirational to me.

As I got older and formed a family of my own, I was able to take valuable learning lessons from her and my mother to add and apply to my life to improve and to create an atmosphere for my children that was productive, positive, and encouraging. It wasn't always easy because first I had to learn how to get out of my own way.

One of the most important things that I had to lean on was God. One of the challenges that I faced as a single mother, with male children, is that there was a completely different approach than what I had been used to. I come from a household with two sisters and one little brother, so it was quite different with me being a mother of five.

I realize over the years that just to have a man in your life is not conducive if he's not going to add value, boundaries, faith, and leadership to add to the mission. Too often women are looking for men to fill the void, but not too often looking for men who are wanting to be an example. We need to start asking God to send us a model man, a man that fits the criteria of the likeness and image of God and it's not a fantasy. There are some really great men in the world, but we have to prepare ourselves so we can be equally yoked and have them come in and take their place. So, I made it my duty to not. bring another man around my children unless he possesses all those attributes and no it's not being realistic or asking for too much when you've been through the fire, you've been tested, and you learn your value because that is when you won't settle for just anything.

Dear Diary,

My much-needed super mommy weekend has officially arrived, and I managed to buy three new, sexy fits. My long-term, long-distance boo had already FaceTimed me twice just to make sure our plans were still on. Between being a full-time nurse and a mom, we have to schedule our free time weeks in advance.

I had my niece and my bonus son coming over after school to watch my daughter for the next two days. I kept it short and simple with my ex, knowing he would love any reason not to drop our son off and not pick our daughter up. As long as the kids knew where and how to find me, then we were all right. I had everything planned out perfectly. I prepped all her Ketogenic meals, washed, and folded all the laundry, and labeled all her medications for better access so it would be a lot easier for everyone. My daughter is 11 years old now and still nonverbal but uses cues to communicate.

Before getting dressed, I decided to take a hot bubble bath. I lit my lavender candles, turned on my 90s slow jams through my Alexa, and stepped into my bath. I started reminiscing about the past few weeks: I worked 48 hours in the COVID-19 units, attended a virtual IEP meeting, and still managed to take my daughter to three specialty appointments. Life wasn't always easy, but we managed.

As I was having my bath, I felt a lump on my right breast. I immediately sat up and started wondering if I really felt anything before attempting to feel it again. My heart sank to the pit of my stomach when I realized it was actually there. There was no pain, but doesn't a lump usually mean a cyst or even cancer?

I was so worried and crying so hard that I had to cancel my date. I knew my boo would be hurt, but he was so understanding. The person who always helped everyone else now needed help.

After our talk, I got dressed and went to my primary care doctor for an emergency breast exam. She asked if I drank caffeine and, if so, how much and how often. I explained that I drank soda daily to boost my energy when I am tired.

My doctor explained that sometimes, it's possible for caffeine to cause lumps in our breast tissue. She suggested that I limit my intake or stop drinking caffeine in general. In the meantime, she gave me a referral to have a mammogram done.

Now it's been two days, and I'm sitting in my bedroom with a house full of kids, thanking God that the lump went away. I'm still going to my scheduled mammogram, but I'm happy I took time for myself, even if my weekend plans ended before they ever started.

Dear Diary,

I have allowed that four-letter word, L-O-V-E, to subconsciously have me waiting and settling in another space of isolation, chaos, and disconnection. My co-parent relationship has shifted to a selfish place where family round tables seldom exist, schedules fluctuate like the weather, and plans get canceled frequently due to unpredictable traffic. I have gone from the baby momma of an inmate to the trucker's wife.

He said this time, the circumstances would better him. I somehow processed this statement to mean better us as a family, but that was not the case. The celebration of his evolution is bittersweet. However, I thought this journey would be easier than prison.

I feel a sense of ungratefulness. We finally have an opportunity to head a two-parent household for our children, but with a career that requires him to be away from home again. One responsibility of being a wife is supporting your husband's dreams, but why does it feel like he's in prison again? There is so much freedom on the road, but the difference in time zones doesn't allow the kids to chat with him much.

I have always recognized patience as the softest form of love. What I am not so sure of is the formula for playing this position. I often feel like the distant lover that Marvin Gaye used to sing about. Most of the time, that two-way street we found love on becomes a lonely highway, as Teena Marie said. I listen to her often – and my other favorite oldies – to numb the down time. I miss the type of music when love was true, the vibes were real, and the energy was positive.

Music replaces the voids and inconsistencies experienced by the trucker's wife. It's the feeling of being single, married, and a mom all at the same time. It may not make sense, but this lifestyle is not for the weak.

There is no such thing as mom preparing breakfast while dad makes sure the kids are dressed and ready for school. No mom packing the lunches while dad warms up the car. No mom heading to ballet class while dad heads to football practice. No mom preparing dinner while dad helps with homework.

Instead, life has pretty much become a 1974 episode of "Wait Til Your Father Gets Home." Imagine trying to raise two sons who know their dad cannot show up at school to resolve a disciplinary issue. Or that the raspiest voice they will hear will be mom's. God forbid I speak in a soprano; they would most likely take it as a joke.

If only their dad could reach out and touch them through video call. I get lucky if T-Mobile phone towers give us service when trying to call their dad. Since he is an Android user, chances are, in certain areas, service isn't available.

Therefore, out comes the super cape of masculinity – or that so-called nagging sound of momma. The voice of reason and teaching, in the tone that I often regret. My daughter looks, waiting on her turn for her mom's gentle love. So many times, I've wished their dad could show up to the school like some superhero right in the middle of my son's antics. Instead, I am always the sacrificial parent, leaving work to surprise him with a strong arm and a single mom face of "you know what time it is."

When I finally feel like I have the household under control physically, mentally, and spiritually, here comes "Disneyland Dad," the truck driver who comes off the road to his family. But he has no concept of the rules, regulations, and boundaries established by a single mom. As a result, he ignores everything, sweeps all the important topics under the rug, and says, "Daddy's home!" Of course, he expects a carpet rolled out for him.

He wants to be bothered with nothing but peace. But what about the issues from the parent-teacher conference? It is always, "Wait until I leave, then give your mom the blues." My kids take advantage of that every time, which is how the pattern of parental dysfunction starts. This is my testimony as the trucker's wife.

But who said being a single mom was bad? If you ask me, I'd rather have one band, one sound in my house, so everyone marches as a unit. It seems like I've failed my children sometimes when trying to juggle both roles. The choices and decisions of parents affect the mental health of children in so many ways. The backpack of the single mom requires a pair of panties that are sometimes not the sexiest, partnered with some Ethika draws (underwear), I guess.

This is especially true when raising boys. The stressors of single mom hood overwhelm family situations sometimes, but there is no other hood that I respect more. So, I encourage mommies who end up single to take the challenge. You can be a mom unapologetically, with no mixed values, morals, or distractions. If the situation is exhausting, chaotic, or toxic, just do it yourself. It beats being the trucker's wife any day. This may be tea to you, but this is my testimony.

Dear Diary,

Lord, being a mother is the most rewarding and fulfilling position I have ever accepted. But how am I supposed to carry the weights and responsibilities that come with it without losing myself? I know I can't protect them from everything in life, and sometimes I question what I actually birthed them into... I question myself about the things I did not see that they would encounter and have to walk in because of who they were directly and indirectly attached to!

I didn't know parenting was generational... I didn't understand that what I chose to entertain would one day come back and knock on each one of their doors to ask for a ransom! I didn't realize the cost! The intentionality of my prayers would have to increase, and the intensity and frequency of those prayers would have to be amplified to a higher degree than what I could ever know! I had no clue this would be such a lonely and winding road that

I would have to walk – sometimes crawl or run – through. Sometimes even blindly feel around in the dark, fall, and get back up.

Oftentimes – at the expense of my sanity – in exhaustion, sleep deprived, depressed, heart in pain and agony, completely void and empty I was unable to see the sun on some of those days! I would wonder how I had ended up in this space and in these foreign places of making decisions and choices that would shape, mold, and form another person's life! My decisions and choices no longer belonged to me and me alone… they had become pregnant with three other life forces that I was accountable and responsible for!

At times, I would just pray that I could make it through the night… through the dark places that I had to navigate through internally to transcend the void I was feeling in my own life. Yet, I still had to feed and clothe little reflections of myself and their fathers.

Father, teach me their love languages so I can listen to their hearts and understand their needs. Show me how to love them in the way you created them to be loved. Help me, help them, walk in their purposes. Help me introduce you as their Father. Open my eyes so I can see outside of the box and past the limitations of being a single mother.

Dear Diary,

A fatherless son has been one of the most difficult assignments I have been given. I have to play mother and father. I wasn't designed to be in the role of a father. I can't teach my son how to be a man. I couldn't even properly potty train him. I had to let my brother demonstrate the correct technique.

There have been numerous ups and downs in this parenting process. My son is very intelligent; he excelled in school. However, his behavior has always been a challenge. He was diagnosed with Attention Deficit Hyperactivity Disorder (ADHD) at the age of four. The medication was a temporary solution to a spiritual problem. After a while, the stimulant medication loses its effectiveness, and we're back to the drawing board. He has been prescribed every medication for ADHD. Some worked, but most didn't. The side effects were persistent. He would lose around ten to twenty pounds when the medication was reintroduced into his body. The insomnia and aggressive behavior were the most troublesome. When he was around thirteen years old, I felt like he had lost his mind. He became so callous and selfish. He was getting suspended from school and started to be disrespectful. No matter how much I disciplined him, his behavior didn't change. I truly felt defeated. I wanted to give up on him due to my frustration and lack of support. His actions were so detrimental that they affected our relationship. I started to develop a strong dislike for my son.

He attended counseling to get to the root cause of his issues. He had mentors. None of it worked. I threw my hands up for a moment and criticized instead of praying. I spoke so many curses over my son's life due to my frustration and anger. I spoke him into incarceration.

I didn't have a relationship with Jesus Christ until

my son was older. Prior to that, I allowed the spirits of rebellion, strife, and confusion to rule and dominate my household. There wasn't any peace. I was so bitter and resentful. I let the enemy have his way in our lives for years because I didn't possess the full armor of God.

I wasn't the best mother. I was dealing with my unresolved issues of abandonment and rejection. I cursed instead of blessed. I discouraged him with my hateful words instead of uplifting him. I would discipline him out of disappointment because his father was absent.

We are now working on restoring our relationship. The word says that the seed of the righteous shall be delivered. His word also says to let the redeemed also tell their story. We overcome him by the blood of the lamb and the word of our testimony. I know that God is going to work it out for the good.

If you don't have anything positive to say, then

don't say it. Seek deliverance, counseling, and healing. Apologize and repent.

Dear Diary,

Today is February 10, 2023, and it's 2:16 pm. I'm sitting here at the office thinking about what I can do today to encourage myself & to edify God at the same time. I'm like, "God, what can I do to be a better mom? What can I do to be a better person? What can I do to be a better daughter? I just want to be better all around." I heard in response, *"Be honest!"*

The best thing you can do to become better is to be honest. Not according to the world, but to be honest according to *my* word. But I asked, "What does that look like?"

He said, *"Look in the mirror and when you look at yourself, see your children. While seeing your children, see the child in you who continues to live for good purpose."*

I have a child in you that's necessary in order for

you to hear me clearly because as an adult & through your experiences that taint your spectrum, you won't hear and see me the way I need you to unless I keep that child in you alive. John 10:27-28 dawned on me: *"My sheep listen to my voice; I know them, and they follow me. I give them eternal life, and they shall never perish; no one will snatch them out of my hand."*

So, I'm sitting here, knowing that my children know my voice like nothing else. What does this scripture mean? What has my voice been to my children? How is the tone of my voice impacting my children when I speak? What is my voice commanding in the atmosphere over my children? I have so many questions, and I believe the answers are in scripture.

I looked into the scripture, and it says that God's voice is honest in His instructions that guide our lives. God tied the scripture together for me by letting me see if, as His child, I don't know His voice, then I do not know His word. This prevents me from being obedient and blocks His help. If I do not know His word, I cannot establish my faith, and that prohibits my trust in Him.

Then came the question: Who can be honest in the absence of trust? Well, no one! So, God is saying that, as a mom, the best thing I can do is be honest and understand by His wisdom the impact of my voice. I have to see it from their perspective and ask myself, "How honest is my voice?"

Is my voice speaking life? I am not talking about the basic, tangible things but what I speak into their hearts. What is my heart speaking to my child? This is what I will be mindful of each day as a single mom. I want to provide help with the sound of my voice; I want to provide encouragement, correction, guidance, and, most of all, love by the word of God and not the world.

Dear Diary,

I am so thankful for my life and the blessings that you bestow upon me through my three life forces. Being a mother is beyond the reach of love that I am familiar with. My introduction of this love through each of my babies has been vastly different!

My firstborn captured my heart irrevocably! How did I get here? What is this space in my heart that is beating so loudly and profoundly for the redemption of life through this part of me that I carried and labored for? Who did you create her to be Abba? Reveal it to me... show me the direction I should go! Send your winds to capture us and set us in the direction and path that we should travel on to be free!

Her purpose was birthed through my expansion. Even in her father's absence, she is loved to my fullest capacity! I vow to be the best mother that I know to be! The internal struggle may exist, but it will not break me!

I will let go of all the things that are blocking me, holding me back, tying me down, and hindering us from moving beyond our captivity. Enlarge my capacity for this journey. Give me multiple layers of provision for the days ahead.

Just when I thought I didn't have any more capacity for love, I gave birth to my son. You showed up and made me realize there was room for more. You have stretched me past the limits of my first love and propelled me headfirst into deep waters. I have deeper depths that I had no idea even existed.

My baby girl, the last of the Mohicans, shocked me to my very core! You are a miracle indeed. Lord, help me! I didn't know I had more! More space in my heart and mind to conceive the thought of loving her in conjunction with the places that had been invaded by my other children. Oh, how you have taken me past all my limitations and inhibitions. I have to hold onto myself because you are so beautiful and delicate to the core.

I thank you Father for being the creator of all things! I thank you for creating three masterpieces out of my chaos. Priceless and valuable to me. Equivocally beyond the more, the totality of me! I have realized all I have to do is partner with the Creator and watch His workmanship speak to me. I hear the song in my head. How deep is your love...it's a new meaning for me.

Dear Diary,

As a single mom, it was my responsibility to care for and protect my little ones at all costs. I didn't want my children to feel like they had to depend on public assistance to live. The curse of poverty had to be destroyed.

I became determined to be an example of the saying, "Hard work pays off." So, I decided to go back to school for cosmetology. I loved doing hair and thought I could set my own hours and still be available for my children. I could also make more money, and we would be able to live and not just survive.

While attending school, I found out I was pregnant with my third child and once again alone to care for them by myself. Halfway through my course, it was almost time for me to give birth to my son. I was out on maternity leave for three weeks and returned to finish the five weeks I had left to graduate. I was determined, and it paid off. I graduated, and all three of my children were there.

Lord, once again, I'm by myself with three children now, struggling to make it and take care of everything. I know you did it before, so Lord, can you please do it again? I need you. I can't do it alone. That was my prayer.

God opened a door for me, and I went to a mass hiring event at Target and got hired. I couldn't wait to start, but I did get sad. Who's going to watch my babies?

My immediate family didn't live close, nor did I have any friends that could watch them. I had to come up with a solution. I could decline the position, or I could create latch key kids and leave them home by themselves until I get off work.

The only solution was number two. So, I had to sit down with my children and explain to them what was going on and what we had to do as a team to make it and do better. I would make sure that dinner was ready for them, and I instructed them not to go outside, answer the door, or use the phone. I told them not to have company over and not to touch the stove.

By us being determined together, we achieved the saying, "Hard work pays off." My children and I were able to go on a mini vacation and make memories. If you are struggling, make Philippians 4:13 your declaration as I did. *"I can do all things through Christ who strengthens me."*

Dear Diary,

When they said I couldn't or I wouldn't, I did. So many times, I wanted to give up, listening to what people were telling me. People were saying that things couldn't be done because they thought I wouldn't change. Well, I proved them wrong by making my children my strength.

I lived in my dad's home to the projects, friends' houses, and back to the projects until I realized it was time for me to stop. I had to listen to my own heart and not others' words. My last straw was when my aunt wanted to control what I did in my own home.

My job at Winn Dixie wasn't cutting it; it wasn't what I needed to raise my children with stability. I was applying for other jobs but still wanted to party; that was my downfall. I couldn't do both and save my children. One day, a recruiter came for my little sister so she could take the test to get into the Army. She wasn't there, and I never knew she wanted to go into the military, so I went and took the test.

The test results came back in a few weeks, stating I could pick my job. It was time for a change. God had answered my prayers for a better life for my family. For the next couple of months, I prepared myself and my family for my time to leave. I had to get my children set up with a family care plan; they were all separated. The time came for me to leave, and I was devastated. My dad cried, and I cried, but the strength that I had came from knowing it would be better when I returned.

Every time I took a test, I knew I had to pass for my kids. I had to complete it for them. I would hear my brother's voice, who was in the military, saying, "Girl, you got this." One time, at 200 pounds, I had to run a seven-minute mile uphill. I hadn't ran since high school, but God, I ran it in less than seven minutes! I knew I had to do it for my kids.

I went through some hard times, but I never gave up. Sending the little money I did receive back home was my goal; it wasn't for me; it was for them. I achieved goals I never thought I could. To see my dad's face at my graduation made me feel so good, but to see my children's faces when we moved overseas and I was able to provide a new life for them was priceless. Too many times, we let other people get in our heads; I let people tell me we couldn't or wouldn't do things. They brainwashed me into believing these things. I have learned not to believe everything I hear.

Do not be so quick to give up on something you've never tried. From one single mother of four and a grandmother of five, we made it, and it was all by the grace of God and the faith I had in him. Encourage yourself to be what you want to be. When I let God lead me instead of the people around me, I achieved goals I never thought I could accomplish.

My little ones gave me the strength to keep pushing. Even today, I do things with my children and grandchildren to push me.

Dear Diary,

As a single mother, you naturally become more than just a mommy to your children. You become a doctor, a nurse, a counselor, an apparatus, a personal chef, and a mediator. You play the good cop and the bad cop at the same time. You are their *everything*.

Your emotions are valid; be gentle with yourself. Yes, being a mother can be rewarding, but it can also be draining. When you wear multiple hats in a single day, it will put a smile on your face, but it can also be frustrating.

To be the sole provider for my girls is amazing yet humbling. God trusted me enough to raise three beautiful girls. God provides for us, and he leads me to resources that help us every day. From giveaways to grants to assistance programs, I couldn't have gotten here today without them and the leading of God. For it will not always be like this; this is only a season. In this place, appreciate it and be grateful, for it could be another way. Keep going and love yourself!

Dear Diary,

As I'm sitting in the doctor's office waiting for my results, there are so many thoughts racing through my mind. Do I keep the baby or have an abortion? How am I going to tell my mama? What is she going to think? Am I like my sisters and nieces? I wasn't a teenage mother, so I'm good, but I still think that I am like them.

When the nurse returned to the room, she revealed that I was indeed pregnant. I wasn't in shock; I was disappointed with myself. I'm a broken, wounded 22-year-old young lady from the projects. I'm the first person in my family to attend college. How could I be so careless? How am I going to take care of a baby who didn't ask to be here or finish college?

I suffered from depression during my pregnancy. I wasn't enrolled in college during this time. I didn't want to gain a lot of weight during the pregnancy, so I mostly ate chicken Caesar salads. My obstetrician was concerned because I wasn't gaining enough weight during the pregnancy. He referred me to a program that assisted mothers-to-be, and I was introduced to an advocate. She would provide counseling, resources, and even attend a few doctor's appointments and Lamaze classes with me. She was very instrumental.

I was working when my water broke. I was more than six hours away from family and friends. I called my mother to tell her what had happened. A friend drove me to the hospital, and I gave birth to my son three weeks early, surrounded by numerous friends, my roommate, my baby daddy, and no family. I felt so alone, although the room was filled with people who were there to support me during this joyous occasion. My mother and sister arrived the following day. I was so excited to see them. I cried like a baby when they left; I felt abandoned.

Motherhood has been a challenge. When I brought my son home from the hospital, I was terrified. I knew I was unprepared and ill-equipped to be a mother. Reality hit me at that moment. I could change diaper with just urine, but when that first soiled diaper happened, I didn't know what to do. Imagine having to wipe and clean a baby boy from under the scrotum, anus, and up his back. I couldn't do it!! My roommate had to change the diaper because I almost vomited everywhere.
When it was time for his first bath, I didn't even know how to bathe him properly. I felt so defeated. I didn't know how to properly care for his umbilical cord or his uncircumcised male part.

As a mom, you need to take care of your mental health and yourself. I had to learn this. It all gets better with practice and time. I couldn't be so hard on myself. I had to ask for help when needed. I had to stop assuming everyone was against me and I had to stop running people away with my negative attitude and self-sabotaging ways.

Dear Diary,

Today is March 10, 2023, and it's currently 12:27 pm. I decided to write something fresh while getting ready to head to Kaiser.

My back has been out the whole week, and it has been excruciating. I'm not sure if this is sciatica or if it's due to spinal spurs, but it has been highly painful, to the point of me being immobile. Some single moms really don't have the help that has been "gifted" to many other mothers. I'm really out here doing it on my own about 94.89% of the time. My children have been truly helpful, even down to the five-year-old. Yet, for me, as a grown woman, it has been a challenge trying to allow my mind to sit so my body can heal. There's always a need that has to be met.

I started to think about the peace of consideration. God never told me to compare myself to another. God does not compare trials and tribulations. He did advise me to please Him and help others through life's changes. What balances this out is having taken the initiative to recognize and welcome my design as an eccentric woman and mother for the foundational platform of my children.

I've never been one to sit back and focus on another mother's issues unless it directly affected me. I just don't see the purpose of looking at another mother's parenting if it wouldn't be useful to my own. I found that, in life, I don't have to go through something in order to learn. God allows me to see through others the things I can take with me along my odyssey of being a single mother, even if it's used later on. I figured I'd take those keys so, should I have to enter that door, I'm already equipped to access it instead of being frustrated, trying to figure out a way. Hell, the key might even be used for the exit!

Even today, I'm comforted as this ailment passes

in not having the desire to compare myself. It started with my very first pregnancy; people would attempt to say certain things out of common nature and societal norms, which I instantly refuted as it didn't sit right with my soul. This is not to say that I won't encounter some of the same afflictions in life as other mothers, but it is to say that just because it happened to you does not mean it'll happen to me.

I learned to see this voyage of motherhood to be my own. The anxieties, stress, and tensions are far less apparent in my life since I chose to defenestrate the demon of comparison.

The scripture for this lesson is 2nd Corinthians 10:12: *"We do not dare to classify or compare ourselves with some who commend themselves. When they measure themselves by themselves and compare themselves with themselves, they are not wise."*

God is the only candidate, and all else are a mere part of the campaign. If you know, you know! Bless up!

Dear Diary,

My life as a single mother began at the tender age of fifteen. Yes, I was a baby, but God blessed me with a beautiful little girl. I was told that I wouldn't be able to make it after having a baby at an early age, but that wasn't true. My mom and grandmother were there for some time until they couldn't be due to their illnesses. But they helped me a lot.

The Lord has plans for my child and me; my dad and his mom (my grandmother) helped by all means. They took custody of my firstborn when my mom got sick, and my grandmother was taking care of her. As life went on, I was blessed with two more beautiful children, having to raise them partially single because their father was incarcerated most of their lives. This left me with a single-income household.

Raising three kids when separated from my oldest

was hard, but I never complained. I always made sure we were always together. The trials of being the main breadwinner were difficult. Daycare was $175 per week, and I had to leave my kids to drive two hours away and make $9 an hour. This was not OK with me. I survived by the grace of God and my father, aunts, grandmother, and their father's side of the family.

Staying with my dad was hard because I had to live under his rules, and I didn't want to disobey him. When I had my last baby, I decided to move out. I wanted to be a grown up, so I moved to what we call the projects. That $50 a month for a two-bedroom was off the chain back then as a young girl with four kids. I got the kids to daycare, went to school to further my education, and worked. Jesus was my fence. I would wake up at 5 AM to get my kids to the babysitter; then, I would go to school and work. I would walk to work unless a classmate took me.

I would do that same routine each day. Cabs would have all my money until tax time when I purchased a car, but it was still hard with gas and daycare. Life was what it was, but by the grace of God and family, we survived. My life as a single mom was not all peachy. I wanted to cry more and more each day, but giving up wasn't an option.

I started doing things no mother wants to do. I was drained for many days and kept going because I had four children to be there for, even though I didn't physically have my oldest. She was with my grannies and dad. If it wasn't for them, I don't know where I would be, knowing that none of their fathers gave me anything. It was the grandparents, aunts, and uncles that helped me raise my kids.

I never thought I would be in this situation, but God brought us out of it. After a failed marriage, I decided to go into the military to better myself for my children. Leaving them was hard, but I knew I had to get away to make a change, so I did.

Every day that I was away, every task that I did, I was thinking about them. They were my strength to keep going.

My faith in God kept my spirits up, and my thoughts of being a better parent kept me above water. God will place you in predicaments where you have to call on him only, and this was my time. After losing my mom, I knew it was time for me to start being the parent she knew I could be.

Thank you to my father and family for being there for me. Just because you have a child young, it doesn't mean you cannot continue.

Dear Diary,

Today, I'm completely overwhelmed. My ten-year-old daughter's emotions are all over the place, and it's causing her to be absolutely insane. Crying because she's mad, she's happy, and she's sleepy; she's a pre-pre-teen! All of this while my youngest daughter wants to nurse every hour, screaming at me and pulling at my shirt. She is making it physically impossible to do anything other than feed her. And let's talk about my five-year-old "flower child," who is so chill and goes with the flow. It's scary. ABC Mouse and a bottle of water, and she's cool.

Meanwhile, I'm managing not to feel overwhelmed, and I'm learning to breathe and take it one moment at a time. When it's too much, prayer and meditation music is my go-to. While reflecting and resetting, I'm reminded that being a single mom is beautiful, exciting, fun, joyous, and rewarding. But sometimes, it's scary, exhausting, lonely, and overwhelming. Your thoughts run away, overlapping emotions, and it causes anxiety and stress. I question my actions and why I'm on this journey of parenthood alone.

I then take a step back, just breathe, and remember to take it one day at a time. To be gentle with myself and know that I'm doing the best I can and God will do the rest.

I have to stay focused on God and remember that I need care, too. I need to take time for myself.

Thank you, Lord, for allowing me to raise three beautiful girls. Thank you for being right by my side.

Dear Diary,

I got a call this morning from my ex's first baby mother. They share a six-year-old. She and I talked for hours and came to a mutual decision to put our differences aside so we could raise our children to know each other. I currently don't even talk to our baby's father, so maybe this will be best for the kids.

I haven't spoken to this nigga in 16 whole days. The last time we spoke, he reached out to get some money that I already didn't have because I was only making $8.50 an hour as an assistant. He said it was so he could make it to my cervical cerclage procedure. Of course, I gave in, and he still made an excuse the day of and didn't show up. Now, he stopped answering altogether.

I had already miscarried our first baby in 2006, which resulted in a D&C. I went into pre-term labor with our son in October 2007, and he passed, too, so stress is the last thing I'm taking on. Today at 1 PM is my ultrasound appointment, and I plan on getting a 3D print of my healthy baby's face. Nothing is standing in my way today, except I still had to ask my mom for bus fare to get there. She gave it to me, but not before saying that I needed to come up with a better plan for my baby's life.

I just moved back here before finding out that I was pregnant again. She's allowing me to share a room with my only brother, who is 10 years younger than me until I get on my feet. So, I don't know how to tell her about the news I received.

The technician ushered me from the exam room down to a big conference room where a bunch of people wearing white coats were already seated across from me. The genetic counselor introduced herself and went on to explain that my baby was showing signs of hydrocephalus. She told me there's increased fluid in its brain. This was a lot to take in, especially because I didn't understand how or why this was happening.

All I wanted was to get a 3D print of my growing baby. They all took turns introducing themselves and giving their take on how our lives would be with this type of injury. Everything was a blur to me until I heard a social worker suggest a hospital-paid abortion. Or placing my baby in a long-term residential house but allowing me to visit. They were concerned that I was only 20 years old, knowing it would be expensive, and I was single.

Without wiping any tears falling from my saddened eyes, I yelled that I was still keeping my baby. I know this means I'll have a lot of research and preparation to do, but I've never backed down from challenges before.

Dear Diary,

Today's been a rough day!

I've been working hard all week. I planned to attend an event and did, but before I left, there was so much that I needed to do. I have to keep a clean house. After going out, I came home with even more things to do. My son depends on me for so many things.

I think back on how I dreamed of being married with a big house for my family. That hasn't happened yet. It's just me here raising my son alone. It's funny because even though he's a boy, he acts just like me. Man, he has my attitude. Some days we bump heads. I often think that, as a mom, I can't speak or relate to some of his needs. There are some needs that I believe only a man can speak or relate to.

I can tell when I take him to the barbershop, and

he's talking to the guys about God knows what; that's what he longs for. He doesn't say it, but I know he wishes that he could be around his dad. I truly know that God is sending someone that will be good not only for me but for him, too. I believe he's going to make up for all the years I had to do it alone.

I never thought this would be my story of raising my kids alone. I don't live with any regret because I've done an amazing job. I told myself that I would be honest with myself about my feelings. I say that because sometimes it really does stink how things are, but I am reminded that it won't always be this way.

Dear Diary,

I didn't think I would make it, but I've survived 18 years. I could think back to when my daughter was just a newborn. I knew she was special then. Her dad left when she was about three years old. Moving forward, I knew the journey would be hard raising her on my own, but I also knew I could do it. Through the years, there were so many struggles, but I had no choice but to grow up.

We often think that children just learn from their parents, but parents can learn from their children, too. My little girl really taught me a lot. More than anything, she taught me to love and give hugs.

There were days I didn't know how I was going to do it. There were also many days where I allowed the pain to blind me, but today I celebrate because we made it. I can't say I made it, but we made it. My daughter graduated high school with honors! We did it! She got accepted into one of the top colleges. Let's not forget to mention that it's an HBCU.

I'm very proud of her. I had to let myself know how proud I was of myself, too. I didn't think I could do it, but I did it. I raised my babies well. I have some amazing children. They're very caring, loving, supportive, and intelligent. I have to give myself a pat on the back because being a mother or being a parent doesn't come with a manual. It's trial and error, but we learn. I've learned that, as the Bible says, I can do all things through Christ that strengthens me (Phil 4:13).

Now my daughter is off to college, which is so mind-blowing. I am the mother of a college student. She's the first generation to attend a four-year university. I can definitely say that she's broken the generational curse!

It was challenging to let my daughter leave home. Now, I get to see her live out what I have imparted into her. I have not been disappointed. It's been a blessing watching her grow into a beautiful woman. That really brings a smile to my face. It makes me want to work even harder so I can continue to lead her in the right direction.

Dear Diary,

It's late, but I feel like writing. I think back to the days when it was as if I was living in hell here on Earth. I was raising a sickly child who was on numerous medications, all while trying to give my little girl the attention she needed. Not to mention fighting through what was going on in my head and having a sick heart.

But fast forward, and by God's grace, my son is only on one medication now! And my daughter is getting ready to graduate high school as an honor student with nine college acceptance letters! Little ole me is watching lives change worldwide because of my testimony of never giving up as a business owner, ministry leader, international radio host, first-time author, and so much more.

I want other mothers to know that it might look crazy now. They may feel like they want to throw in the towel. All hell is breaking loose. But they were built for this, and one day their story will change someone's life because God is faithful!

Dear Diary,

So, me and the kids went to the museum today and we had so much fun. I am so thankful for my babies. I love planning family dates with them. Sometimes we go out to dinner. Sometimes we go to the movies, or we have picnics.

I always try my best to make sure that I spend quality time with them because I know working to put food on the table and clothes on their backs is not enough. They need me, so I've created the space for that. I've created a space where I turn my phone off and give them my undivided attention. I listen to their thoughts, their wants, how they feel, what makes them happy, and what makes them sad.

We have to listen to our children and create safe spaces for them. We have to let them know that their feelings are valid.

When is family time? Whenever it is, we have to be sure that everything else is off-limits. Even when they're young, we have to help them understand what is going on instead of not talking to them at all. Maybe not all the personal stuff, but the times when you have to work late, etc.

I had to learn to explain to them why I'm frustrated. Being a parent doesn't come with a guide, but we should try our best to give our children the best parts of ourselves. That may look like seeking community, finding single mom groups, and joining empowerment groups.

It was important for me to be around those that would be a blessing to me on multiple levels and not tear me down! I have to continue to pray and do my best!

Dear Diary,

One thing I know, for sure is that being a single mom comes with a lot of pressure, the pressure of expectancy and trying to understand what that looks like for you and your children. Sometimes that can be very challenging when you have not been given the proper tools necessary to embrace your own weaknesses as an individual.

In the society that stripped us from our culture and broke us down throughout the generations were the singleness of a woman, and the lack of a father is the norm. So, what do we do when we get lemons, we improvise, we strategize, and we recognize whatever the next step is to be productive and provide for children.

So many of us are so used to being in survival mode. We have missed the mark in so many areas. I want to really learn how to identify and live life, so we take those things, and what we have learned over the years, and some of us implement them in positive ways and some struggle to see the true essence and power and being a mother.

My goal is to grow each and every day from the things that I have learned and have experience through life lessons. My goal is to be kind to myself, and to take a moment to accept that I am single, but there is a greater mission in myself. I will take the time to learn a new skill that will add value to my life that will bless the children.

Sometimes it's hard to even think about the blessings when you have been so used to the struggle but there's a benefit to being a single mother. There's a power, there's a sense of liberation to an extent when you know that you have the authority to make better decisions for you and your child It's hard work, but God will help you and his spirit will rest upon you in the midnight hours even if you have to cry yourself to sleep, know that you are not alone, and God is working things out for your favor in your singleness.

I had to be mindful of the conversations I had with other women who may be going through a similar situation and be mindful to keep my heart and mind open to all positive conversation and information that will have an impact on my healing process. As a single mom, there's definitely some trauma and some healing needed.

We can't be so quick to jump into another relationship. I am worthy of love; I am worthy of more than I have ever imagined.

My children are worthy of a father, who will love and respect them and their mother. One who will do his best to not only provide but to be a spiritual anchor and who can lead and direct the family.

About the Authors

Browniesha Blackman

A multi-faceted woman of purpose, Transformation Coach Browniesha Blackman has carved her own lane of success built on her personal battles with grief and self-worth with the help of her spiritual gifts. As the CEO & Founder of TransformUrLyfe Coaching & Consulting LLC, Browniesha creates digital and seminar spaces for transformative recognition, healing, and empowerment. She is the founder of the *"Break Free" Healing Experience Workshop* which encourages people to push past their challenges and break free of barriers holding them back.

Browniesha has made significant strides in transformative consulting & entrepreneurship and shows no signs of slowing down. She continues to live out her dreams of helping others through her pen. Browniesha's first solo literary project, *Metamorphosis: The Transformation*, is a transparent memoir chronicling the traumatic experiences of her life and transforming those pains into purpose. The book became an Amazon international bestseller and inspired Browniesha to empower others through literary healing.

She produced an anthology, *The Healed Woman*, with 11 other individuals sharing their story of healing. In June 2022, she released another anthology, *Dear Dad*, with 22 other individuals who wrote letters to their fathers expressing the matters of their hearts. Browniesha is also a co-author in *Brutal Courage: The Remix*, an anthology with over 20 individuals telling their story about overcoming trauma.

Taking her purpose to the page has resulted in Browniesha being a four-time bestselling author. Her work has even shined on-screen in a featured guest spot in the documentary, "The Rhythm of Blue." A portion of her story was also acted out in the monologue "Blue is the Color of Happiness."

Of the many talents Browniesha has, her most fulfilling role is that of a mother. A mother of three, Browniesha created The Arri Foundation, a nonprofit organization after the passing of her daughter, Arrionna. She is dedicated to assisting grieving families who have lost babies and small children all over the world.

Browniesha is a living testament that dreams can come true no matter the starting circumstances. Her ability to transform her pain into a business of passion is inspiring to all those who are privileged to come into contact with mother, business owner, evangelist, mentor, and coach Browniesha Blackman.

Barbara Rankin-Williams

Barbara Rankin-Williams was born in Monroe, Louisiana and later relocated to Los Angeles, California, with her grandmother. She is a single mother of seven and grandmother of nine.

Barbara is a certified addiction specialist who works with the homeless, mental health, substance abuse user and formerly incarcerated population. She has over 15 years of experience in this field. Because of her past life experiences, Barbara is empathetic and genuinely concerned about the welfare of others without her priority being for profit.

Barbara recently received the Beacon of Hope Award and in 2015 she received the Humanitarian Award from Los Angeles County. Her dream is to continue to move forward in life and be a light and inspiration to those who feel defeated and are battling being in darkness.

Dr. Malika M. Gordon

Dr. Malika M. Gordon is a healthcare professional with 20 years of experience. She is a graduate of Florida Agricultural and Mechanical University, where she earned her Doctor of Pharmacy degree. Malika is passionate about educating people about the importance of medication adherence. She is in the process of developing her consultation agency. She wants to incorporate medicinal and holistic alternatives to treat diseases.

She wants to contribute to closing the gap in health disparities in the underserved communities. Malika understands that wholeness means addressing trauma, disappointment, and mistakes. She desires for others to be set free from oppression, condemnation, guilt and shame. She hopes her transparency will free another mother from the feeling of failure.

Malika is the mother of two adult children. She resides in Florida. Malika enjoys traveling, volunteering, spending time with family and friends, watching basketball and football, cooking, and dancing.

Elonda Ingram

Prophet Elonda Ingram is the visionary of the Touch and Agree Ministries. She answered God's calling into the ministry in 1991. She was ordained as a Missionary and Evangelist at the beginning of her ministry and she was ordained twice as a Prophet; however, she recognizes one throughout her ministry.

God pulled Prophet Ingram out of the local churches to do his Kingdom work. As a result, as she began to walk in faith and do the work of the Lord, other prominent leaders began to recognize early on that there was a higher calling as a Prophet upon Elonda Ingram's life. Most importantly, God dealt with Prophet Ingram on numerous occasions to answer the call to serve as voice for the voiceless; the hope for the hopeless; and the healer for the unhealed.

Prophet Ingram is a dynamic, servant leader, serving as messenger for our Heavenly Father to pray, encourage, uplift, and warn the people. Touch and Agree Ministries is the name appointed to Prophet Ingram in 2014. The Lord gave Prophet Ingram the instructions and the name of the ministry in a dream. Touch and Agree Ministries has a prayerline and occasionally provides Bible Study to the global communities at large as the Lord leads.

A self-published author, Prophet Ingram also makes anointing oils, according to Exodus 30:22-33. She makes her anointed oils with the best ingredients as inspired by her mother who made oils for over 25 years.

Jeri Gregory

Jeri Gregory is a single mom of three beautiful girls. She is an entrepreneur, freelancer, and the creator of *The Single Mom's Diary*. This space was created for mothers to lay their hair down and be free. Jeri also includes mommy hacks and will soon release a mommy guide. She does all her work from the privacy of her home.

Jeri has learned how to manage working and handling the daily task of her motherly duties. Though being a single mother can be challenging, she makes the effort to provide her girls with home cooked meals and activities to keep the space of bonding and communication. On this journey she was inspired to help other mommies just breathe and embrace the good, the bad and the ugly.

Jeri began writing and video blogging to encourage and relieve herself from frustration. Being creative and worshiping is also her go to. Jeri created *The Single Moms Diary* to allow mommies to find the beauty in their single mother journey and bring awareness to how special and amazing they are as a mother! As she prepares to launch *The Single Mom's Diary"* support group, she wants every mother to feel safe and free to express their journey.

K. Verily Me Brazwell

She goes by her brand name *Author Verily Me*, yet her given name is Kemoyne Brazwell and as bold as her name, she is indeed a marvelous work. Kemoyne is a California native with a fervor for the ways of God, free from the limits of titles to share the "Good News." Many have called her WOG (woman of God), Evangelist, Missionary, Minister but she prefers servant in reverence to the Most High God.

Kemoyne is a lexophile who maintains a reticence for learning. She has always loved school and believes life in and of itself gives a new lesson each day. She's book smart, street-savvy, and considered a leader. Even as a lassie, Kemoyne had a conscientious character that allowed her to speak in a manner that provokes thought, so much so that at times it garnered the possibility of a tail turning! Kemoyne had an "out of the mouth of babes" journey that only grew with prudence into the voyage of her yesterday, today, and tomorrow ministry.

Kemoyne is a woman of faith, a mother, and what she likes to call "lifepreneur" which circumscribes all things life and the option of ownership, a sage, scribe, hope-dealer, chef, poet, singer, an actress, dancer, artist, mentor, and a person who appreciates the gift of life. She learned early that above all these things nothing matters more than how God views her, and in that alone she moves accordingly. Kemoyne is Author Verily Me, a daughter of the Triune God Almighty.

Kadana Bryant

Prophetess Kadana Bryant is an ordained Prophetess, Pastor, Minister, Evangelist and Missionary. She Pastors alongside her Husband, Apostle Leonard Bryant Sr., of "Storming the Gates of Hell Ministries." She is the CEO / Visionary of *Pressured Made Diamonds Mentorship Program*, Vessels of Worship Praise Dance Ministry School, N His Presence Prayer Ministries, N His Image Beauty Salon and Bundles of Joy Daycare.

Kadana is a licensed Cosmetologist, Medical Assistant, and Phlebotomist. As a Survivor of Domestic Violence, she is a Domestic Violence Advocate and Mental Health Coach and a three-time bestselling Author, and the Visionary of *Unbroken Vessel*, an anthology about surviving domestic abuse. She is truly a Virtuous Woman of God.

With a Prophetic call upon her life, she has been a Vessel of Excellence that God has used to exemplify his greatness and to further His Kingdom. She walks in integrity, she is a powerful prayer warrior, dedicated intercessor and an exceptional praise and worshipper. She is full of love and compassion for everyone, through love and kindness have I drawn thee. She is a blessing to everyone she meets. Hell trembles, for she has stormed the gates of hell, lifting up the name of Jesus.

Prophetess Kadana has a thorough understanding of God's grace and mercy, loves to tell her story and gives all the Glory to God. Her mission is simple: save the lost at any cost. God has moved in her life in so many ways, so if anyone is wondering whether God is still working miracles, just look at the living testimony of this Woman of God, who God raised from the dead.

LaKeisha M. Trimm

LaKeisha Trimm-Green is the mother of four beautiful young adults who have blessed her with five beautiful grandchildren. She is a U.S. Army Veteran and still serves her fellow veterans with pride and dignity.

LaKeisha is one of six founders of Alpha Delta Omega Military Sorority Inc. She has a degree in Health Administration, Business Administration and Health Information Technologies/ Medical Front Office. She is the owner of Moments Like This Coaching and Counseling Services LLC., and she is a motivational speaker and grief counselor.

In her spare time, LaKeisha enjoys riding motorcycles, traveling, helping others, family time, reading and journaling. She has co-authored two international bestselling books. She's a 2x Amazon Bestselling Author and 2x international bestselling Author.

LaShaundra Douglas

LaShaundra Douglas is a native of Birmingham, Alabama. She is a Kingdom builder, anointed influencer, a mother of three beautiful children, a daughter, a sister and a friend. She is an aspiring author, an identity coach, a motivational speaker, an entrepreneur, and a business owner.

Pushing others into their destiny by unmasking and unmuting the identity thief in their lives is her life work and passion. Her mission is to teach others how to birth purpose out of trauma and pain. She is a lover of learning and good food.

Roshanda Y. Casteel

Roshanda has a wide range of experience. Her greatest accomplishment is being a mother of seven beautiful children. Her mission is to encourage women & families across the world who have suffered the loss of a loved one with mental illness, through suicide, or diabetes, and families with open child protective services cases.

As an inspirational speaker, life coach, and family mentor, Roshanda empowers and serves her community to the airwaves. She is the host of *So Divine* radio and the host of The Bridge Family Wellness show on accelerated radio iHeart tuners and Springer's and the after-party West radio show. She was nominated by wigging out radio of the city of Los Angeles for positive and most influential in the community in 2017.

Roshanda has been featured in community magazines for her accomplishments and her influence in leadership for mentoring adults and youth. She was acknowledged by the Latino Chamber of Commerce for her support and services throughout the community. She has been an inspirational entrepreneur building up communities, restoring a process outlook on family relationships, her topics such as Community Building Restoration provide information on various topics to all of her listeners.

Roshanda is very proud of her nonprofit organization *Progressive Family Solutions* that has be serving the cities of Long Beach and Compton, California. Roshanda's mission is to help rebuild family relationships by providing resources such as economic development, men and women support groups, youth advocacy and family advocacy programs, a positive example for her peers and her community.

Sha'Dawn Sampson, LPN

Sha'Dawn was born and raised in West Baltimore, Maryland. She is the oldest of four children born to her mother who was raped as an preteen, yet still decided pro- life and raised her baby as best she could as a 14 year old child turned single-mother.

Sha'Dawn has always been a fan of reading and writing short books while growing up. You'd often find her posted in trees laying across the strongest branch with her journals. After school daily she would rush home to copy pages out of encyclopedias and other historic books to encourage her imagination and increase her growing mind and penmanship.

Sha'Dawn began working at the age of 15 years old as a storyteller/librarian's assistant for a program at her senior high school, reading stories to groups of children at the Enoch Pratt Free libraries around Baltimore city. She also assisted with creating PSAs on late night local TV about using protection when being sexually active. She taught college students at Morgan State University and adults about the importance of STI/STD and HIV prevention at Baltimore city department of health.

Sha'Dawn has always been a leader in her own right. In 2007, she began her journey with raising and nurturing her children to be as independent as possible. In 2018, she relocated out of Maryland to the state of Virginia to provide a safer upbringing for her children. Excelling in college, she went on to become a Licensed Practical Nurse. The soon-to-be author has surely beaten the odds set against her from the very start.

Shaunee' Breaux

Shaunee' Nicole Breaux is a creative, born and raised in Los Angeles, California. At a very young age she was recognized as highly innovative and gifted in her academics. It was also very early in life that Shaunee' demonstrated strong leadership qualities that naturally provoked her lifelong passion for working with children.

Before graduating high school Shaunee organized her first community group amongst her peers. The Westside Dominettes Youth Drill Team and Drum Squad was established in 1991 to give at risk youth an outlet from gangs and other adversities. Through this organization and many other youth development projects, Shaunee' has inspired others to win in life.

Shaunee' started her career in Early Childhood Education in 1993. She gave birth to her second child and third child but did not let that deter her from going after her goals. She finished her AA degree at LA Southwest College, then enrolled in an accelerated undergraduate program at Springfield College, where she earned her bachelor's degree in human services in 2004. Shaunee' enrolled in her last round of school, earning her master's degree in organizational leadership/ management in 2008.

Shaunee' is currently the founder and Director of Bizee Bodeez Incorporated, a 501c3 organization whose vision is keeping children rooted with experiences that nurture the whole child. Aside from her youth development efforts, Shaunee' is the author of two children's books: *Zoom Room* and *True Finds Her Shoes*. She currently provides Early Education consultations and professional development training for early childhood learning programs. Ms.Breaux strives daily to continue to develop positive alternatives for youth so she can be a part of the change in the community that she would like to see.

Tanya Denise

Tanya Denise is the Founder & Executive Director of the International Association of Women Authors (IAWA), the world's leading global network for women who write. She is a self-published, international, best-selling author, a master anthologist, and book coach. Tanya has been writing since she was a young girl, beginning her journey with poetry and short stories, then gradually growing into newsletters, newspapers, independent magazines, journals, and books.

In 2018, Tanya published her first book and launched Love Wins Publishing (www.lovewinspub.com), to assist new and aspiring writers in becoming published authors. She has since published more than 53 of her own works and she has helped more than 350 writers become first-time published authors.

Tanya has a heart for helping others. Her passion has led to the receipt of several community awards, including Woman of the Year by the Antelope Valley Ad Hoc Committee on Education. She holds a Bachelor of Science degree in Communication, a post baccalaureate certificate in Marriage & Family Therapy (MFT), and she is currently pursuing education in psychology.

Tanya's purpose is to utilize her proven faith in God to serve as a catalyst to help others heal and operate in their gift(s). Her mission is to use her gift of writing to help women and empower them to walk in their purpose. A mother of two amazing sons, she currently resides in Southern California. Tanya enjoys traveling the world and her favorite places thus far include Monaco and Abu Dhabi.

For more information, speaking engagements, bulk book orders, to contact the lead author, or to contact any of the co-authors in this project, please visit:

www.brownieshablackman.com

www.ingramcontent.com/pod-product-compliance
Lightning Source LLC
Chambersburg PA
CBHW032129090426
42743CB00007B/530